Pedro's Big Mexican Adventure

Children's Learn Spanish Books

Speedy Publishing LLC
40 E. Main St. #1156
Newark, DE 19711
www.speedypublishing.com

Let’s learn the Spanish Alphabet.

ENGLISH	SPANISH
a	*ah*
	Pronunciation

Trace the letters.

ah ah ah ah

Rewrite the letters.

ENGLISH	SPANISH
b	*bay*
	Pronunciation

Trace the letters.

bay bay bay bay

Rewrite the letters.

ENGLISH	SPANISH
c	***say***
	Pronunciation

Trace the letters.

say say say say

Rewrite the letters.

ENGLISH	SPANISH
ch	***chay***
	Pronunciation

Trace the letters.

chay chay chay chay

Rewrite the letters.

ENGLISH	SPANISH
d	*day*
	Pronunciation

Trace the letters.

day day day day

Rewrite the letters.

ENGLISH	SPANISH
e	*ay*
	Pronunciation

Trace the letters.

ay ay ay ay

Rewrite the letters.

ENGLISH	SPANISH
f	*ay-fay*
	Pronunciation

Trace the letters.

ay-fay ay-fay ay-fay

Rewrite the letters.

ENGLISH	SPANISH
g	*hey*
	Pronunciation

Trace the letters.

hey hey hey hey

Rewrite the letters.

ENGLISH	SPANISH
h	ah-chay
	Pronunciation

Trace the letters.

ah-chay ah-chay ah-chay

Rewrite the letters.

ENGLISH	SPANISH
i	ee
	Pronunciation

Trace the letters.

ee ee ee ee

Rewrite the letters.

ENGLISH	SPANISH
j	*hoh-tah*
	Pronunciation

Trace the letters.

hoh-tah hoh-tah hoh-tah

Rewrite the letters.

ENGLISH	SPANISH
k	*kah*
	Pronunciation

Trace the letters.

kah kah kah kah

Rewrite the letters.

ENGLISH	SPANISH
I	*ay-lay*
	Pronunciation

Trace the letters.

ay-lay ay-lay ay-lay

Rewrite the letters.

ENGLISH	SPANISH
ll	*ay-yay*
	Pronunciation

Trace the letters.

ay-yay ay-yay ay-yay

Rewrite the letters.

ENGLISH	SPANISH
m	*ay-may*

Pronunciation

Trace the letters.

ay-may ay-may ay-may

Rewrite the letters.

ENGLISH	SPANISH
n	*ay-nay*

Pronunciation

Trace the letters.

ay-nay ay-nay ay-nay

Rewrite the letters.

ENGLISH	SPANISH
ñ	ayn-yay
	Pronunciation

Trace the letters.

ayn-yay ayn-yay ayn-yay

Rewrite the letters.

ENGLISH	SPANISH
o	oh
	Pronunciation

Trace the letters.

oh oh oh oh

Rewrite the letters.

ENGLISH	SPANISH
p	***pay***
	Pronunciation

Trace the letters.

pay pay pay pay

Rewrite the letters.

ENGLISH	SPANISH
q	***koo***
	Pronunciation

Trace the letters.

koo  koo 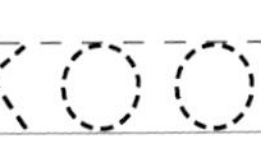

Rewrite the letters.

ENGLISH	SPANISH
r	air-ay

Pronunciation

Trace the letters.

air-ay air-ay air-ay air-ay

Rewrite the letters.

ENGLISH	SPANISH
rr	airr-ay

Pronunciation

Trace the letters.

airr-ay airr-ay airr-ay

Rewrite the letters.

ENGLISH	SPANISH
s	ay-say
	Pronunciation

Trace the letters.

ay-say ay-say ay-say

Rewrite the letters.

ENGLISH	SPANISH
t	tay
	Pronunciation

Trace the letters.

tay tay tay tay

Rewrite the letters.

ENGLISH	SPANISH
u	oo
	Pronunciation

Trace the letters.

oo oo oo oo

Rewrite the letters.

ENGLISH	SPANISH
v	bay chee-kah
	Pronunciation

Trace the letters.

bay chee-kah bay chee-kah

Rewrite the letters.

ENGLISH	SPANISH
w	***bay doh-blay***
	Pronunciation

Trace the letters.

bay doh-blay bay doh-blay

Rewrite the letters.

ENGLISH	SPANISH
x	***ah-kees***
	Pronunciation

Trace the letters.

ah-kees ah-kees ah-kees

Rewrite the letters.

ENGLISH	SPANISH
y	ee-gree-ay-gah

Pronunciation

Trace the letters.

ee-gree-ay-gah ee-gree-ay-gah

Rewrite the letters.

ENGLISH	SPANISH
z	say-tah

Pronunciation

Trace the letters.

say-tah say-tah say-tah

Rewrite the letters.

Let's learn some common Spanish words.

ENGLISH	SPANISH
family	*la familia*

Trace the words.

la familia la familia

Rewrite the words.

ENGLISH	SPANISH
parents	*los padres*

Trace the words.

los padres los padres

Rewrite the words.

ENGLISH	SPANISH
father	***el padre***

Trace the words.

el padre el padre

Rewrite the words.

ENGLISH	SPANISH
mother	***la madre***

Trace the words.

la madre la madre

Rewrite the words.

ENGLISH	SPANISH
son	***el hijo***

Trace the words.

el hijo 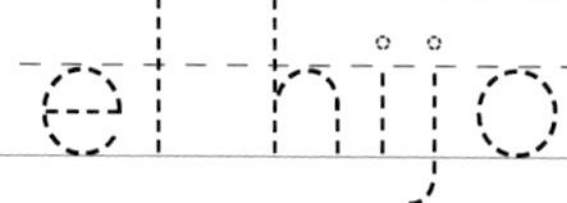 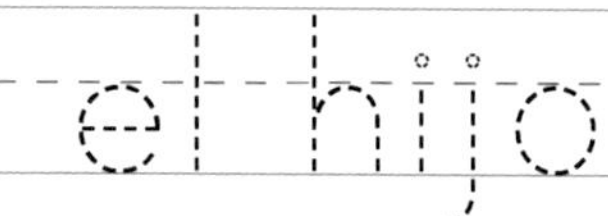

Rewrite the words.

ENGLISH	SPANISH
daughter	***la hija***

Trace the words.

la hija 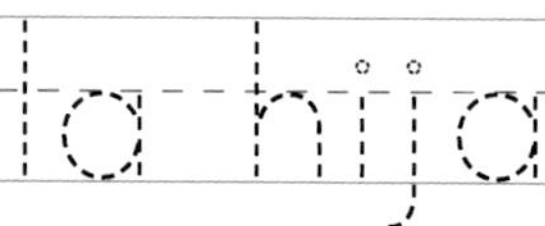 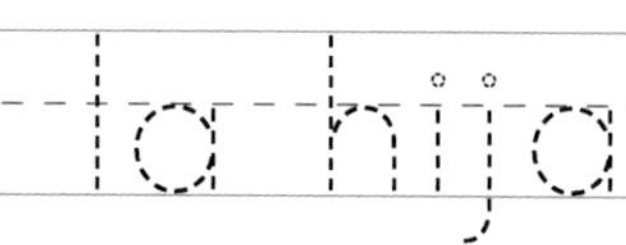

Rewrite the words.

ENGLISH	SPANISH
children	***los hijos***

Trace the words.

los hijos los hijos

Rewrite the words.

ENGLISH	SPANISH
brother	***el hermano***

Trace the words.

el hermano el hermano

Rewrite the words.

ENGLISH	SPANISH
sister	***la hermana***

Trace the words.

la hermana la hermana

Rewrite the words.

ENGLISH	SPANISH
grandfather	***el abuelo***

Trace the words.

el abuelo el abuelo

Rewrite the words.

ENGLISH	SPANISH
grandmother	*la abuela*

Trace the words.

la abuela la abuela

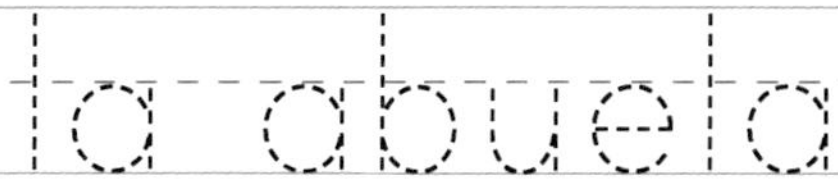

Rewrite the words.

ENGLISH	SPANISH
grandson	*el nieto*

Trace the words.

el nieto 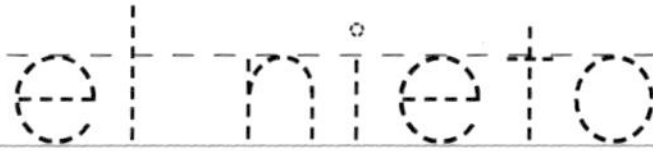 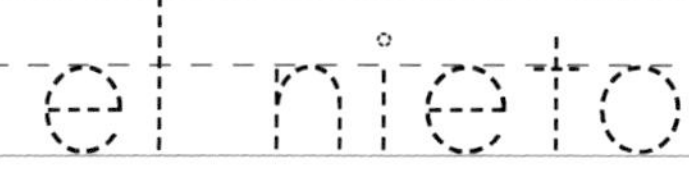

Rewrite the words.

ENGLISH	SPANISH
granddaughter	***la nieta***

Trace the words.

la nieta la nieta la nieta

Rewrite the words.

ENGLISH	SPANISH
uncle	***el tío***

Trace the words.

el tío el tío el tío

Rewrite the words.

ENGLISH	SPANISH
aunt	***la tía***

Trace the words.

la tía la tía la tía

Rewrite the words.

ENGLISH	SPANISH
nephew	***el sobrino***

Trace the words.

el sobrino el sobrino

Rewrite the words.

ENGLISH	SPANISH
niece	***a sobrina***

Trace the words.

a sobrina a sobrina

Rewrite the words.

ENGLISH	SPANISH
cousins	***los primos***

Trace the words.

los primos los primos

Rewrite the words.

ENGLISH	SPANISH
baby	***el bebé***

Trace the words.

el bebé 

Rewrite the words.

ENGLISH	SPANISH
teenager	***el adolescente***

Trace the words.

el adolescente

Rewrite the words.

ENGLISH	SPANISH
dog	***el perro***

Trace the words.

el perro el perro el perro

Rewrite the words.

ENGLISH	SPANISH
cat	***el gato***

Trace the words.

el gato el gato 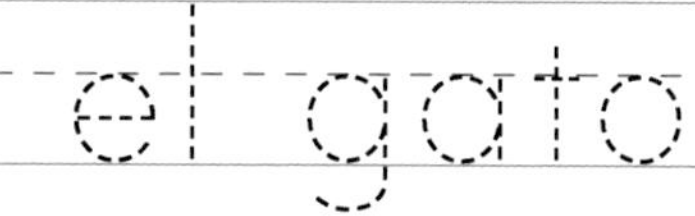

Rewrite the words.

ENGLISH	SPANISH
bird	***el pájaro***

Trace the words.

el pájaro el pájaro

Rewrite the words.

ENGLISH	SPANISH
fish	***el pez***

Trace the words.

el pez el pez el pez

Rewrite the words.

ENGLISH	SPANISH
horse	***el caballo***

Trace the words.

el caballo

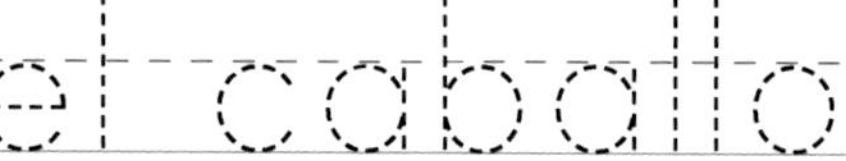

Rewrite the words.

ENGLISH	SPANISH
goat	***la cabra***

Trace the words.

la cabra la cabra

Rewrite the words.

ENGLISH	SPANISH
pig	***el cerdo***

Trace the words.

el cerdo el cerdo

Rewrite the words.

ENGLISH	SPANISH
cow	***la vaca***

Trace the words.

la vaca la vaca la vaca

Rewrite the words.

ENGLISH	SPANISH
rabbit	*el conejo*

Trace the words.

el conejo el conejo

Rewrite the words.

ENGLISH	SPANISH
turtle	*la tortuga*

Trace the words.

la tortuga la tortuga

Rewrite the words.

Let’s learn some basic Spanish phrases.

ENGLISH	SPANISH
How are you?	¿Cómo está usted?
	koh-moh ay-stah oo-sted

Trace the phrase.

¿Cómo está usted?

Rewrite the phrase.

ENGLISH	SPANISH
What is your name?	¿Cómo se llama usted?
	koh-moh say yah-mah oo-sted

Trace the phrase.

¿Cómo se llama usted?

Rewrite the phrase.

ENGLISH	SPANISH
Good afternoon!	***¡Buenas tardes!***
	bway-nahs tard-ays

Trace the phrase.

¡Buenas tardes!

Rewrite the phrase.

ENGLISH	SPANISH
See you soon.	***Hasta pronto.***
	ah-stah prohn-toh

Trace the phrase.

Hasta pronto.

Rewrite the phrase.

ENGLISH	SPANISH
You're welcome.	*De nada.*
	day nah-dah

Trace the phrase.

De nada.

Rewrite the phrase.

ENGLISH	SPANISH
Thank you (very much).	*(Muchas) Gracias.*
	(moo-chahs) grah-see-ahs

Trace the phrase.

(Muchas) Gracias.

Rewrite the phrase.

ENGLISH	SPANISH
See you tomorrow.	***Hasta mañana.***
	ah-stah mahn-yahn-ah

Trace the phrase.

Hasta mañana.

Rewrite the phrase.

ENGLISH	SPANISH
Congratulations!	***¡Felicitaciones!***
	feh-lee-see-tah-see-oh-nehs

Trace the phrase.

¡Felicitaciones!

Rewrite the phrase.

Made in the USA
Las Vegas, NV
02 April 2023